tourism TATTLER

Issue 07 (JULY) 2015

PUBLISHER
Tourism Tattler (Pty) Ltd.
PO Box 891, Umhlanga Rocks, 4320
KwaZulu-Natal, South Africa.
Website: www.tourismtattler.com

EXECUTIVE EDITOR Des Langkilde
Cell: +27 (0)82 374 7260
Fax: +27 (0)86 651 8080
E-mail: editor@tourismtattler.com
Skype: tourismtattler

MAGAZINE ADVERTISING
ADVERTISING DIRECTOR Bev Langkilde
Cell: +27 (0)71 224 9971
Fax: +27 (0)86 656 3860
E-mail: bev@tourismtattler.com
Skype: bevtourismtattler

SUBSCRIPTIONS
http://eepurl.com/bocldD

BACK ISSUES (Click on the covers below).

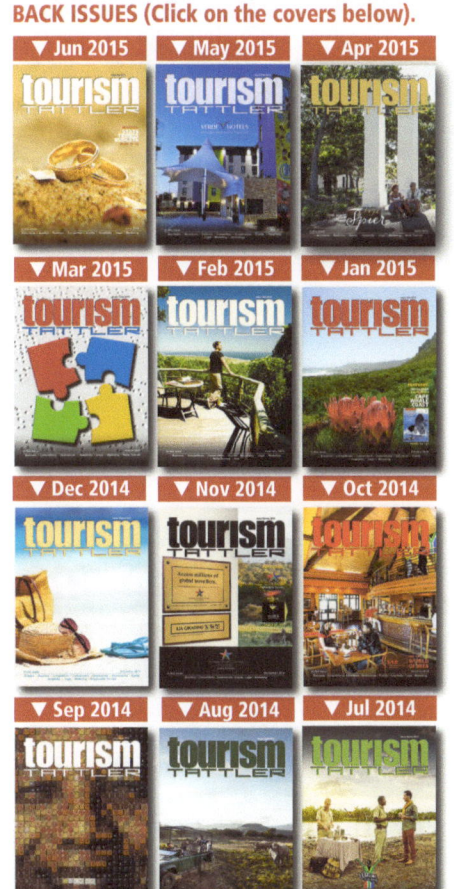

▼ Jun 2015   ▼ May 2015   ▼ Apr 2015
▼ Mar 2015   ▼ Feb 2015   ▼ Jan 2015
▼ Dec 2014   ▼ Nov 2014   ▼ Oct 2014
▼ Sep 2014   ▼ Aug 2014   ▼ Jul 2014

Contents

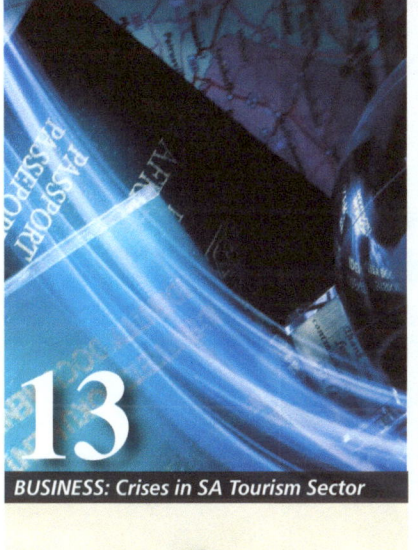

13
BUSINESS: Crises in SA Tourism Sector

18
EVENTS: Conscious Conferencing

22
EVENTS : Ghosts of Grahamstown

23
MARKETING: Expatria's Tourism Potential

IN THIS ISSUE

EDITORIAL CONTRIBUTORS

Adv. Louis Nel
Alexandra Dodd
Charlene Nieuwoudt

Des Langkilde
Elzaan Rohde
Jennifer Nagy

Kanyisa Ndyondya
Martin Jansen van Vuuren
William Purbrick

MAGAZINE SPONSORS

Sports & Events Tourism Exchange

27 - 29 October 2015
Protea Hotel Fire & Ice! Menlyn, Tshwane

SAVE THE DATE

NEW CITY
NEW FORMAT
NEW FOCUS

A B2B platform aimed at positioning South Africa as a Sports and Events Tourism Destination.

The annual Sports and Events Tourism Exchange, now in its fifth year, is the only event of its kind in Southern Africa and provides a platform that brings together businesses from the sports, events and tourism industries, SETE encourages collaboration between these sectors over a two-day conference, two-day table top exhibition and networking events.

Sports & Events Tourism Exchange (SETE) will see new and exciting changes including the change of the exhibition format. SETE has launched the Invitation-Only Table Top Exhibit this year which will be more affordable and efficient for focusing on important Buyer & Exhibitor Meetings and concluding business deals.

SETE 2015 will also be focusing on Golf Tourism as one of the key Sports Tourism Industries and will be targeting 10 - 15 International Golf Buyers.

The International Hosted Buyer Programme will again welcome pre-selected high calibre buyers to visit South Africa and interact with exhibiting companies at SETE. 30 buyers from the international sports and events tourism industries will be targeted as well as specific golf tourism buyers.

For more information contact:
Rene Staack
Rene@ThebeReed.co.za
+27(0) 11 549 8300

www.sportsandevents.co.za

Organised by:

Host City Partner:

 /SETE.ZA   @SETE_ZA

To love, laughter & happily ever after

Visit our website for
WINTER WEDDING
specials!

BrightLiquidLight

Guvon Hotels & Spas

ALL SUITE ON 14TH • ASKARI GAME LODGE & SPA • BUSH WILLOW TENTED CAMP
FAIRWAY HOTEL, SPA & GOLF RESORT • GLENBURN LODGE & CHICAMA SPA
KLOOFZICHT LODGE & SPA • UMBHABA LODGE

Central Reservations: 08611 08611 48866 • cro@guvon.co.za
www.guvonhotels.co.za • www.guvonspas.co.za

Accreditation

Official Travel Trade Journal and Media Partner to:

The African Travel & Tourism Association (Atta)

Tel: +44 20 7937 4408 • Email: info@atta.travel • Website: www.atta.travel

Members in 22 African countries and 37 worldwide use Atta to: Network and collaborate with peers in African tourism; Grow their online presence with a branded profile; Ask and answer specialist questions and give advice; and Attend key industry events.

National Accommodation Association of South Africa (NAA-SA)

Tel: +2786 186 2272 • Fax: +2786 225 9858 • Website: www.naa-sa.co.za

The NAA-SA is a network of mainly smaller accommodation providers around South Africa – from B&Bs in country towns offering comfortable personal service to luxurious boutique city lodges with those extra special touches – you're sure to find a suitable place, and at the same time feel confident that your stay at an NAA-SA member's establishment will meet your requirements.

Regional Tourism Organisation of Southern Africa (RETOSA)

Tel: +2711 315 2420/1 • Fax: +2711 315 2422 • Website: www.retosa.co.za

RETOSA is a Southern African Development Community (SADC) institution responsible for tourism growth and development. RETOSA's aims are to increase tourist arrivals to the region through. RETOSA Member States are Angola, Botswana, DR Congo, Lesotho, Madagascar, Malawi, Mauritius, Mozambique, Namibia, Seychelles, South Africa, Swaziland, Tanzania, Zambia and Zimbabwe.

Southern Africa Tourism Services Association (SATSA)

Tel: +2786 127 2872 • Fax: +2711 886 755 • Website: www.satsa.com

SATSA is a credibility accreditation body representing the private sector of the inbound tourism industry. SATSA members are Bonded thus providing a financial guarantee against advance deposits held in the event of the involuntary liquidation. SATSA represents: Transport providers, Tour Operators, DMC's, Accommodation Suppliers, Tour Brokers, Adventure Tourism Providers, Business Tourism Providers and Allied Tourism Services providers.

Southern African Vehicle Rental and Leasing Association (SAVRALA)

Contact: manager@savrala.co.za • Website: w

Founded in the 1970's, SAVRALA is the representative voice of Southern Africa's vehicle rental, leasing and fleet management sector. Our members have a combined national footprint with more than 600 branches countrywide. SAVRALA are instrumental in steering industry standards and continuously strive to protect both their members' interests, and those of the public, and are therefore widely respected within corporate and government sectors.

Seychelles Hospitality & Tourism Association (SHTA)

Tel: +248 432 5560 • Fax: +248 422 5718 • Website: www.shta.sc

The Seychelles Hospitality and Tourism Association was created in 2002 when the Seychelles Hotel Association merged with the Seychelles Hotel and Guesthouse Association. SHTA's primary focus is to unite all Seychelles tourism industry stakeholders under one association in order to be better prepared to defend the interest of the industry and its sustainability as the pillar of the country's economy.

International Coalition of Tourism Partners (ICTP)

Website: www.tourismpartners.org

ICTP is a travel and tourism coalition of global destinations committed to Quality Services and Green Growth.

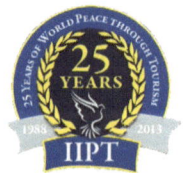

International Institute for Peace through Tourism

Website: www.iipt.org

IIPT is dedicated to fostering tourism initiatives that contribute to international understanding and cooperation.

OTM India 2015

Website: www.otm.co.in

OTM is India's biggest travel trade show, in the largest travel market in India – Mumbai.

The Safari Awards

Website: www.safariawards.com

Safari Award finalists are amongst the top 3% in Africa and the winners are unquestionably the best.

World Travel Market

WTM Africa - Cape Town in April, WTM Latin America - São Paulo in April, and WTM - London in November. WTM is the place to do business.

World Youth Student and Educational (WYSE) Travel Confederation

Website: www.wysetc.org

WYSE is a global not-for-profit membership organisation.

World Travel Awards

Website: www.worldtravelawards.com

Established in 1993 WTA rewards the very best in travel. WTA's global media partner network has a monthly readership of 1.7 million and a TV audience reach of 90 million.

World Luxury Hotel Awards

Website: www.luxuryhotelawards.com

World Luxury Hotel Awards is an international company that provides award recognition to the best hotels from all over the world.

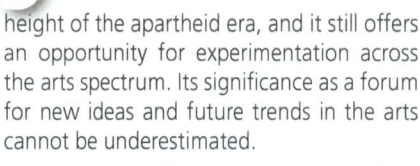

Our cover for July is dedicated to the National Arts Festival – a major tourist attraction, and an important event on the South African cultural calendar. It is also the biggest annual celebration of the arts on the African continent.

Starting at the end of June/beginning of July, it runs for 11 days and is held in the small university city of Grahamstown, which is situated in the Eastern Cape, 130km from Port Elizabeth.

The cover image is from Masote's Dream – an inspiring journey into the life of one of South Africa's most iconic classical musicians, Matlhaela Michael Masote who, during the apartheid era, founded the first black youth orchestra. The Soweto Youth Orchestra, now named the Soweto Symphony Orchestra, gave birth to one of the most internationally acclaimed musical groups to come out of South Africa, the Soweto String Quartet

The Festival consists of a Main and Fringe programme both administered by the National Arts Festival Office.

The programme comprises drama, dance, physical theatre, comedy, opera, music, jazz, visual art exhibitions, film, student theatre, street theatre, lectures, craft fair, workshops, tours (of the city and surrounding historic places) and a children's arts festival.

The event has always been open to all regardless of race, colour, sex or creed. As no censorship or artistic restraint has ever been imposed on works presented in Grahamstown, the Festival served as an important forum for political and protest theatre during the height of the apartheid era, and it still offers an opportunity for experimentation across the arts spectrum. Its significance as a forum for new ideas and future trends in the arts cannot be underestimated.

A committee of experts in the various disciplines selects the content of the Main programme. The planning process takes into account what is available locally and from outside South Africa. Three considerations that influence decisions are the artistic merits of any submission, the creation of a varied and balanced programme, and the costs involved.

Today, the Fringe is on an equal footing with the Main Festival. Seasoned performers and famous directors can just as easily be found on either programme, and a slot on the main programme one year does not preclude a return to the Fringe the next. The distinguishing feature of the Fringe is that it is open to all and exempt from the selection process that applies to the Main programme.

In this edition, Dr Alexandra Dodd writes about a few of the many productions at this year's National Arts Festival that will be raising up the troubled ghosts of the 19th century in her article 'Speaking with Ghosts in Grahamstown' (see pages 20 to22).

As usual, we have our regular subject features in this edition (see content on page 3). it

Enjoy your reading!

Yours in Tourism,

Des Langkilde. *editor@tourismtattler.com*

'Jilted' by the Cape Academy of Performing Arts. Rejected, spurned, abandoned, deserted, dumped, ditched, cast aside and left in despair. The wedding day came, but not the bridegroom. Jilted at the altar with no happily ever after. CAPA returns for their 12th season at the Grahamstown Festival with a new captivating production filled with dance, drama and song that will keep audiences entertained and inspired.

Competition

'Like' / 'Share' / 'Connect' with these Social Media icons to win!

The winning 'Like' or 'Share' during the month of **July 2015** will receive a
Candola Papilio Lantern with the compliments of
Livingstones Supply Co – *Suppliers of the Finest Products to the Hospitality Industry*.

Win

Livingston Supply Company

Tourism Tattler

Competition Rules: Only one winner will be selected each month on a random selection draw basis. The prize winner will be notified via social media. The prize will be delivered by the sponsor to the winners postal address within South Africa. Should the winner reside outside of South Africa, delivery charges may be applicable. The prize may not be exchanged for cash.

July Prize: Candola Papilio Lantern

Candola products are based on a simple, but unusually functional principle which guarantees many practical advantages for restaurants and hotels in the everyday application. Instead of conventional candles, Candola uses a bottle, which is filled with a special totally odourless mineral oil.

The wick soaks up the mineral oil from the container and delivers a candle light without smoke and soot. Thus, there is no melted wax as with candles - and consequently no wax residue. Right to the very last drop of oil, the lamp looks as if it was being used for the very first time

Another advantage for restaurants. The oil bottle is hidden under a decorative sleeve. This also guarantees a positive safety side effect. When the lamp tips over the flame goes out immediately. However, apart from these purely functional aspects, the success of Candola is based on the product development. Candola lamps are available in many different models and designs.

Congratulations to our Social Media winner for June 2015

Winner

Falaza Game Park & Spa has been selected as our **June 2015** winner for their **@FalazaGamePark** 'follow' on **Twitter**. Falaza Game Park will receive a **SOY LITE HAMPER** with the compliments of **Livingstones Supply Co – *Suppliers of the Finest Products to the Hospitality Industry*.**

About Falaza Game Park & Spa: Privately owned Falaza Game Park and Spa offers Luxury Tented accommodation and an array of authentic bush experiences in the lush indigenous setting of Hluhluwe.

Neighbouring the World Heritage Site of St Lucia, Falaza is near the renowned Hluhluwe-Imfolozi Game Reserve (boasting the African 'Big Five'), the fascinating corals and dive sights of Sodwana Bay, with endless activities and excursion opportunities within a close radius.

At the lodge guests can indulge in pampering spa treatments, or enjoy exhilarating game viewing by foot, boat or in open 4×4 vehicles.

For more information visit
www.falaza.co.za

About Falaza Game Park & Spa's Prize:
The SOY LITE hamper cotains the following:

1 x Sensual Massage Body Candle
(Pure soybean oil with Ylang Ylang & Rosewood)

2 x small Moisturizing Candles
(100% pure soybean oil. Aromatherapy benefits, Biodegradable & non-toxic)

1x Travel Candle
(Aromatherapy Travel Candle with Geranium, Jasmine and Rose)

1 x Lip Balm
(Organic peppermint Oil)

60 SECONDS ABOUT world travel market

World Travel Market, Senior Director, Simon Press previews WTM 2015.

Tell us about WTM 2015?

WTM 2015 will be the best yet. Total participants for the event grew to 51,500 in 2014 and we expect even more to be coming through the doors of ExCeL – London between Monday 2 and Thursday 5 November 2015.

- WTM 2015 will see the WTM Festivals return after a successful debut to celebrate WTM's 35th event last year
- Furthermore, the Wellness programme – introduced at WTM 2014 – has been expanded to include The Wellness Lounge on the Wednesday and Thursday of the event
- The WTM Bloggers' Speed Networking will also be expanded following a successful debut last year, and
- A Taste of ILTM at WTM will be expanded for WTM 2015 to include international buyers.

How much business can exhibitors expect to conduct?

WTM 2014 saw more than 1.1 million on-stand meetings facilitate more than **£2.5 billion in industry deals**. This year we expect even more business will be conducted, thanks to the number of new initiatives I've outlined. One of the best ways for exhibitors to meet new buyers and sign deals is to attend WTM's Speed Networking sessions, which take place on Monday and Thursday mornings.

What will the event programme look like at WTM 2015?

There will be more than 100 sessions taking place at WTM this year across a comprehensive range of subjects including Aviation, Hotels, Responsible Tourism and Women in Travel. For the first time there will be a gastronomy programme. The hugely popular WTM Captains of Industry, WTM Ministers' Summit and World Responsible Tourism Day will also return.

Which exhibitors should we look out for?

World Travel Market always has the biggest brands in the travel industry exhibiting and WTM 2015 will be no exception. Major airlines at the event include **Etihad Airlines, Kuwait Airlines** and **Thai Airways International.**

Major hotels chains exhibiting include **Rotana** and **Jumeirah Hotels**.

Furthermore, I'm delighted to be able to announce **Mexico** as WTM's Premier Partner for 2015 as part of the Year of Mexico in the UK and the UK in Mexico.

Where can buyers and visitors register for WTM 2015?

Visit **www.wtmlondon.com/register**

DID YOU KNOW?

1 MORE THAN 1.1 MILLION meetings take place at WTM

2 51,500 ATTENDEES from 186 countries at WTM

3 £2.5 BILLION of new business is generated at WTM

4 You can meet 5,000 EXHIBITORS from across the world at WTM

5 There are more than 9,100 WTM Buyers' Club members in attendance

6 MORE THAN 38 travel industry sectors are represented at WTM

7 MORE THAN 17,000 attendance at WTM's conference programme

8 Including more than 8,000 UNIQUE VISITORS

9 The Travel Tech Show at WTM is the UK's LARGEST TECHNOLOGY EVENT

10 WTM's visitor audience has grown by MORE THAN 20% over the last five years

---

Discover the world

2 - 5 November 2015 / ExCel London

Register now
wtmlondon.com

Official Media Partner

Official Premier Partner

world travel market

2 - 5 November 2015 • London

South African Credit Card Fraud Increases

The South African Banking Risk Information Centre (SABRIC) is concerned over the increase in card fraud. The banking industry's gross fraud losses due to South African issued credit card fraud increased by 23% from R366m in 2013 to R453.9m during the period January to September 2014, writes **Kalyani Pillay**.

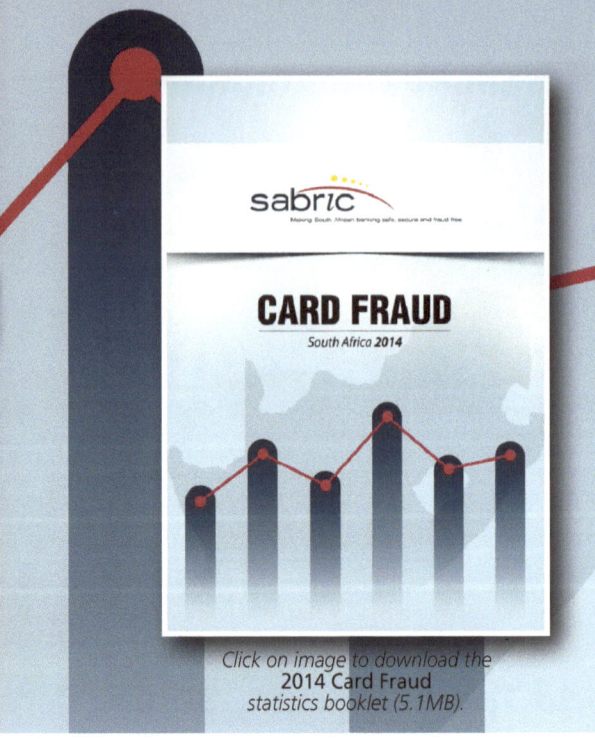

Click on image to download the
2014 Card Fraud
statistics booklet (5.1MB).

SABRIC CEO, Kalyani Pillay said the biggest contributor to the increase had been False Application fraud which saw a very significant increase from R6.2m in 2013 to R78.3m in 2014.

Of all fraud perpetrated on cards acquired through false applications, 88% of the transactions occurred in South Africa. SABRIC found that criminals misuse the online application channels provided by Banks, by using false details to open multiple credit card accounts. Consequently, they then obtain legitimate cards and PINs.

SABRIC was pleased to announce that counterfeit credit card fraud losses inside South Africa decreased by 12% from R55.1m in 2013 to R48.4m in 2014. To the contrary though, Card Not Present fraud committed within South Africa increased by 21% from R56.7m in 2013 to R68.9m in 2014.

The losses associated with debit card fraud also showed an increase of five percent from R117.7m to R123.5m in 2014. The majority of the debit card losses are related to counterfeit card fraud and most of the transactions occurred within South Africa. When debit cards are used outside of the borders of South Africa a high percentage of the cards are used in neighbouring countries such as Lesotho, Namibia, Zimbabwe, Mozambique and Botswana.

Credit card fraud is most prevalent in the Provinces of Gauteng, the Western Cape and KwaZulu-Natal as they collectively accounted for 88% of all credit card fraud losses in South Africa. These provinces also recorded the highest number of skimming devices retrieved. From 2005 to September 2014 a total of 1 377 handheld skimming devices were recovered by either SAPS or bank investigators, with 74 of these seized between January and September 2014.

The majority of handheld skimming devices were recovered in Gauteng (38), KwaZulu-Natal (13) and the Western Cape (9).

Card skimming involves the illegal copying of encoded information from the magnetic strip of a legitimate card by means of a card reader, and this could occur either at ATMs or points of sales. "We urge bank customers to adhere to ATM safety tips such as not accepting assistance from anybody at the ATM and not letting their cards out of their sight when transacting", said Pillay.

Card Not Present (CNP) fraud is still a major contributor to the overall losses on South African issued cards, according to the current fraud trends. CNP fraud continues to experience an increase and the majority of the card fraud transaction take place at foreign merchants.

Whilst counterfeit card fraud still remains problematic, the banking industry is pleased that current information shows a downward trend. This could be attributed to the roll-out of Chip & PIN. The banking industry is however concerned with the increasing threat of stolen card fraud. Cards are swopped in the vicinity of the ATM and cash withdrawals are done fraudulently soon thereafter but before the card holder notices that the card has been stolen and takes action to stop the card. The industry is happy to report that false applications for credit cards have dramatically decreased.

Tips to avoid falling victim to card fraud:

- Be cautious of strangers offering help as they could be trying to distract you in order to get your card or PIN.
- Keep your transaction slips and check them against your statement to spot any suspicious transactions which must be queried with your bank immediately.
- If your card is retained, do not leave the ATM before you have cancelled your card by calling your Bank's call centre using your own mobile phone.
- Never let the card out of your sight when making payments and if possible insert the card into the POS device yourself.
- Do not ask anyone to assist you at the ATM, not even the security guard or a bank official. Rather go inside the bank for help.
- If you are disturbed or interfered with whilst transacting at the ATM, your card could be skimmed by being removed and replaced back into the ATM without your knowledge. Cancel the transaction and immediately report the incident using your Bank's Stop Card Toll free number which is displayed on the ATM or on the back of your bank card. **it**

Download the 2014 Card Fraud statistics here.

About the author: *Kalyani Pillay is the CEO of the South African Banking Risk Information Centre (SABRIC).*

About SABRIC: *SABRIC is a NPF company formed by South African banks to support the banking industry in the combating of crime. Its principle business is to detect, prevent and reduce organised crime in the banking industry through effective public private partnerships. SABRIC co-ordinates inter-bank activities aimed at addressing organised bank related commercial and violent crime and acts as a nodal point between the banking industry and others, in respect of issues relating to crime.*

For more on SABRIC visit www.sabric.co.za

Managing Credit Card Fraud in Tourism

The tourism industry is a popular target for credit card fraud, according to a leading payment services provider – but there are ways to manage the risk, writes **Elzaan Rohde**.

"Accommodation establishments like hotels, guesthouses and B&Bs are especially vulnerable when it comes to last-minute bookings," says PayGate head of business development Brendon Williamson. "Online booking services usually close at least 12 hours ahead, so when someone discovers at lunchtime that they need a room for that same night, the establishment has to take their credit card details over the phone or by email and process the payment manually. That means they lose out on all the fraud checks that are built in to an online checkout process."

"Of course most last-minute bookings are legitimate, and accommodation establishments have to put their customers first," adds Williamson. "But fraudsters know how the system works so this is a popular tactic for them - and they're often very charming individuals. They check in with a false ID and a stolen premium credit card, enjoy VIP hospitality and leave in the morning with nobody any the wiser. They can also be very convincing in getting the establishment to accept a third party payment on their behalf. The establishment might only find out they've been defrauded months later, when they get a chargeback notification from their bank because the real owner of the credit card has complained."

Williamson says PayGate's enhanced PayBill service allows businesses to accept credit card payments outside of their online booking portal, but with all the security checks still in place. "Whoever is taking the booking can easily create a bill and email it to the customer via our Merchant Portal. A secure payment link is included so the customer can click and pay instantly via a secure payment gateway. It's so quick it can all be done during a single phone call."

The system provides peace of mind for customers as well as for businesses, says Williamson. "Many customers aren't willing to give their credit card details over the phone, because they know it could create an opportunity for someone to clone their card. This way the establishment front desk never needs to know the card details until the customer actually checks in -- and the card is always in the presence of the cardholder."

For the business, the entire payment process is all managed securely by PayGate, says Williamson. All transactions are tracked so the business owner can easily check how many bills have been issued and which customers have paid - and send personalised reminders at the click of a button."

Williamson says PayBill is especially powerful when used together with a fraud protection system like PayGate's PayProtector. "The establishment can be confident that the card has been checked against lists of known stolen cards as well as a number of other security checks. This reduces their chargeback risk and ensures that there is a detailed audit trail." **it**

About the author: Elzaan Rohde is an Account director at DUO Marketing + Communications.

About PayGate: PayGate is a payment service provider that offers online retailers simple, effective services to accept electronic payments, which can be a very complex part of running a business. It offers merchants connections to multiple acquirers and fully manages the technical connections and relationships with the banks, card, and payment networks. It also offers risk management services with payment notifications, settlement reports and fraud protection. PayGate is linked to more than 70 banks in over 30 countries and has been providing secure, reliable online payment services since 1999. Its immediately accessible services help businesses of all sizes stay on top of the continuously evolving world of online payments.

For more on PayGate visit www.paygate.co.za

SATIB Health & Wealth brings you the
Tourism & Hospitality Pension Fund

Legislation regarding a National Social Security Fund (NSSF) will soon be implemented in South Africa, enforcing a compulsory combined contribution to pension savings by both employers and employees. The SATIB Tourism & Hospitality Pension Fund, backed by Momentum, enables employers and employees to begin building up their monthly contributions over a three year period to a point where they are meeting the criteria for exemption from contributions to the NSSF.

Benefits include:

- Slow, **manageable build-up** of monthly contributions
- Benefits of scale for the tourism & hospitality industries
- Costs will also decrease as the fund grows
- **Flexible funds**
- Risk-specific funds selected for employees per **age band**
- **Employee's personal fund details available online**
- **Automatic coverage, without medicals**, up to the medical free limits set by the fund
- **FREE Will preparation for all clients!**

For more information, please contact us:

T +27(0)10 591 5555 | **E** satib@attoohjhb.co.za

www.satib.com   **www.attooh.co.za**

Reg no: 2008/022289/23 | attooh! Health and Wealth CC is an Authorised Financial Services provider FSP 24401 | Council of Medical Schemes: ORG 4001

ADMINISTERED BY

SATSA 2015 Conference Golf Day

Date: Thursday 13 August
Time: 08H00 to 12H30
Venue: Montagu Golf Course, Fancourt

Shotgun tee off at 08h00. Montagu, named after the Montagu pass, was originally designed by Gary Player and is a much celebrated parkland course. It has been ranked as the number-one golf course in South Africa in the past and is currently ranked as No. 6 (Golf Digest Rankings 2014). Montagu is at the heart of Fancourt, with its glorious parkland layout, covering large tracts of varying terrain on rolling land. Its beauty is enhanced by mature trees, flower beds, shrubs and water hazards that provide a colourful contrast to the landscape.

The warm-up area, featuring a full-length range and a chipping and bunker practice area, is available to all golfers before play. There is also a golf academy and pro-shops.

Price: R700 (including green fee and cart share)

OUT OF THE FIRE:
WORKING TOGETHER FOR GROWTH

JOIN US AT THE
2015 SATSA CONFERENCE
AS WE EMERGE FROM THE CHALLENGES OF THE PAST YEAR TO FORGE OUR NEW GROWTH PATHS!

DATE: 13-15 AUGUST 2015 • VENUE: FANCOURT, GEORGE, GARDEN ROUTE
ENQUIRIES: pa@satsa.co.za • Tel: 011 886 9996

ISSUE DRIVEN TOPICS INCLUDE:

- Conserving Africa's Wildlife: Beyond the debates - moving into action
- Adventure Tourism – a sleeping giant
- The USA – working better and smarter in our second largest source market
- The Great Rate Debate – BAR v. STO
- The Role of the Tour Operator
- Transformation: going back to basics and new approaches
- The Twin Challenges of Seasonality and Spread
- Responsible Tourism – shifting focus to real issues

SATSA
Southern Africa Tourism Services Association
B⊘NDED

*KEY NOTE ADDRESS BY MINISTER HANEKOM *NETWORKING *QUALITY SOCIAL PROGRAMME

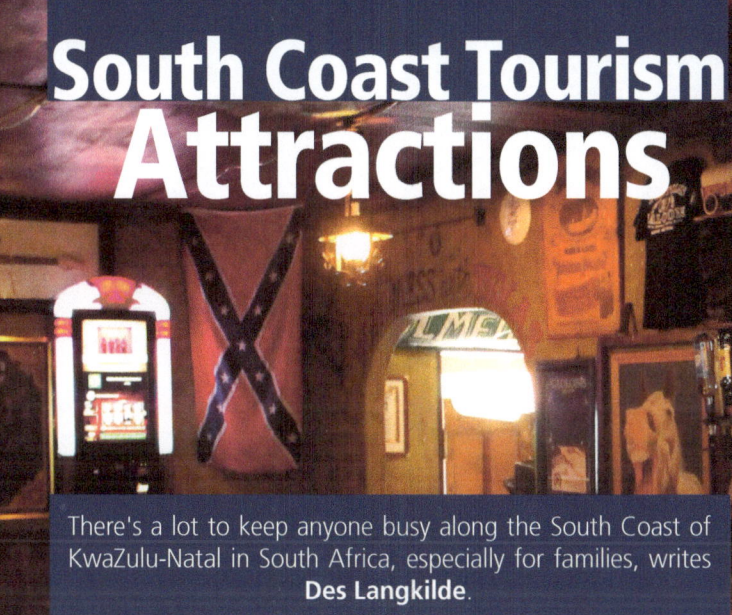

South Coast Tourism
Attractions

There's a lot to keep anyone busy along the South Coast of KwaZulu-Natal in South Africa, especially for families, writes **Des Langkilde**.

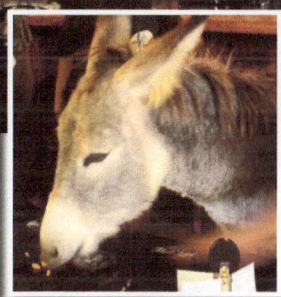

Last month I wrote about the activities that I experienced during my jam-packed post-Indaba media FAM trip itinerary hosted by Ugu South Coast Tourism. Namely Fun Boat Rides with C-Freaks, Beach Horse Rides with Selsdon Park Estate, and Zip Lines with Lake Eland Game Reserve. This month, I'll cover a few of the tourist attractions, which abound along the KZN South Coast.

S'khumba Crafts

S'khumba Crafts is a leather workshop, studio and coffee bar situated between Ramsgate and Southbroom. Each piece of hand-crafted leather ware, which includes shoes, sandals, belts, bags, and a variety of decor and accessory items, is designed and handcrafted by Brian and Karen Bernstein on the premises, using only top-quality vegetable-tanned cowhide.

The indigenous setting of the establishment is like an enchanted forest, as one ambles down the rustic path to the showroom and coffee shop, that serves ice cold beer and homemade treats.

For more information call +27 (0)39 316 8212.

Pistols Saloon

Situated on Old Main road, Ramsgate, Pistols Saloon is really a pub and restaurant but the sheer number of wild-west cowboy bric-a-brac adorning the walls and just about every surface makes this an interesting museum. A regular patron at the bar is Huckleberry the donkey - his party trick is drinking Coke (from the can).

There's a lot for kids to see and explore as well as a selection of arcade style games. For adults there are regular music shows (country music of course) and a real Western bar, complete with an old piano.

For more information click here or call +27 (0)82 871 1241.

Mac Banana

Mac Banana cannot be missed - it jumps out at you with bright yellow signage on the National Road between Palm Beach and Munster. To simply label it as a tourist attraction would be an under statement - it literally has everything for a family outing - from the Banana Café and Pancake Bar to the largest and food emporium that I've come across, which has a cheese room, fresh fruit and vegetables, cut flowers, a vast range of canned goods and preserves, dairy products, sweets and confectionery, a small beach shop and a wine cellar.

Then there's over 20 activities, including the 'Mac Barnyard' for animal petting, a large walk-in butterfly dome, a giant trampoline, pony riding, a paintball combat zone, quad and mountain biking, a mini-golf course, and an art gallery.

Despite all its entertainment and good food (the pancakes and milkshakes really are amazing), Mac Banana is actually a working Banana Farm. Organised educational and scenic tours around the farm with a knowledgeable guide can be arranged by prior appointment.

For more information click here or call +27 (0)39 319 1033.

Next month I'll be reporting on the accommodation and cuisine to be found along the KZN South Coast.

SATSA Southern Africa Tourism Services Association **BONDED***

Grant Thornton

Market Intelligence Report

The information below was extracted from data available as at **01 JULY 2015**. By **Martin Jansen van Vuuren** of **Grant Thornton**.

ARRIVALS

The latest available data from **Statistics South Africa** is for **January to February 2015***:

	Current period	Change over same period last year
UK	85 693	0.78%
Germany	53 144	-7.99%
USA	38 147	-8.67%
India	10 999	-17.80%
China (incl Hong Kong)	12 633	-41.41%
Overseas Arrivals	383 893	-9.79%
African Arrivals	1 159 370	-6.46%
Total Foreign Arrivals	1 558 928	-7.40%

HOTEL STATS

The latest available data from **STR Global** is for **January** to **May 2015**:

Current period	Average Room Occupancy (ARO)	Average Room Rate (ARR)	Revenue Per Available Room (RevPAR)
All Hotels in SA	62.2%	R 1 094	R 680
All 5-star hotels in SA	63.7%	R 1 995	R 1 270
All 4-star hotels in SA	61.7%	R 1 031	R 636
All 3-star hotels in SA	61.0%	R 867	R 529
Change over same period last year			
All Hotels in SA	0.6%	5.9%	6.6%
All 5-star hotels in SA	0.3%	7.8%	8.1%
All 4-star hotels in SA	0.9%	5.6%	6.6%
All 3-star hotels in SA	-1.4%	7.4%	5.9%

ACSA DATA

The latest available data from **ACSA** is for **January** to **April 2015**:

Change over same period last year	Passengers arriving on International Flights	Passengers arriving on Regional Flights	Passengers arriving on Domestic Flights
OR Tambo International	-1.4%	-2.6%	6.8%
Cape Town International	6.6%	3.1%	5.5%
King Shaka International	-0.9%	N/A	3.8%

CAR RENTAL DATA

The latest available data from **SAVRALA** is for **January to March 2015**:

	Current period	Change over same period last year
Industry rental days	4 373 919	-2%
Industry utilisation	71.8%	-1.5%
Industry Average daily revenue	1 352 463 563	1%

WHAT THIS MEANS FOR MY BUSINESS

The data from Statistics South Africa confirms that international tourism has declined significantly. The rest of the data for the first quarter of 2015 shows that domestic business tourism is still continuing. This results in growth in arrivals on domestic flights but do not translate into growth in hotel occupancies or car rental utilisation. The growth in hotel room rates and car rental industry revenue is mostly nominal growth i.e. related to inflationary growth of around 5% to 6% with little or no real growth (anything above 5% to 6%).

Note that African Arrivals plus Overseas Arrivals do not add to Total Foreign Arrivals due to the exclusion of unspecified arrivals, which could not be allocated to either African or Overseas.

For more information contact Martin at Grant Thornton on +27 (0)21 417 8838 or visit: http://www.gt.co.za

South African Tourism sector in crisis

Government's 'Unfriendly approach' to the Visa regime is negatively impacting African and Overseas tourist arrivals to South Africa, reports **Grant Thornton**.

South Africa's Tourism sector is entering its first serious crisis stage as Stats SA's Q1 figures reveal a bleak 6% decline in total foreign tourist arrivals to South Africa for the period ending 31 March 2015. Grant Thornton Advisory Services attributes this decline to a number of factors deterring tourists from travelling to SA, including the Ebola pandemic in West Africa, economic decline in some source countries and the implementation of SA's new immigration regulations.

"The 6% decline recorded in foreign tourist arrivals for the first three months of 2015 equates to a loss of 150 000 tourists, compared to the same period recorded last year. This is a decline of 1600 tourists – or four jumbo jets - per day," says Lee-Anne Bac, Director, Advisory Services at Grant Thornton. "A loss of this magnitude in foreign tourist arrivals is unprecedented. We have never seen such dire levels of decline in the last 21 years of our tourism history." See table below.

This all comes at a time when South Africa's weak currency should be a factor that encourages foreign tourism.

Statistics South Africa (Stats SA) releases monthly foreign tourism arrival data. The report records total foreign tourist arrivals per month, by source country, purpose of visit and mode of transport. Tourist arrivals are defined as visitors who stay in the country for at least one night, excluding travellers who are in South Africa on transit. Tourists include holiday makers and business travellers.

Grant Thornton Advisory Services calculates the direct spend lost to the SA economy as a result of the 150 000 tourist decline, to be R1,6 billion. Bac adds that this loss of foreign tourists excludes the levels of growth that South Africa should have experienced during the same period.

"If we had experienced modest growth of 5% for the quarter, then the total number of foreign tourist arrivals to end March 2015 would have been 2,6 million. So, if we include the expected growth expectations in our estimations, South Africa actually lost 265 000 foreign tourists (and not 150 000) in the first three months of the year and therefore the loss of direct spend in our economy (Foreign Direct Investment) would have been R2,8 billion," she continues.

For the first quarter of 2015, there was a decline in foreign tourist arrivals from the majority of overseas markets to South Africa. Tourist arrivals from the UK bucked the overall trend showing an increase of 5% for the quarter. Overall, tourist arrivals from overseas markets ▶

	Percentage decline Q1 2015/14	Number of arrivals Q1 2015
Total Tourists to SA	-6%	2.29 million
Overseas Tourists to SA	-7%	590 000
African Tourists to SA	-6%	1.7 million

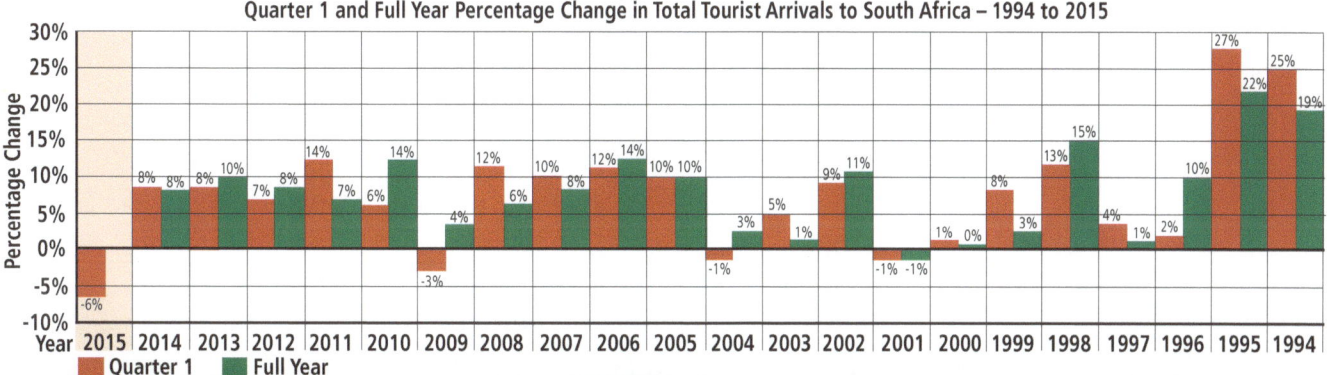

Quarter 1 and Full Year Percentage Change in Total Tourist Arrivals to South Africa – 1994 to 2015

South African Tourism sector in crisis (cont'd)

declined by 6.8% during Q1 2015 according to Stats SA's data, with big declines recorded from the following markets:

- Russia down 47%
- Brazil down 34%
- China is down 38% (the first quarter includes the Chinese New Year, a time of the year when the Chinese normally travel extensively)
- India down 13%.

Tourist arrivals from Africa dropped 5.6% in total for the first quarter period of 2015, with significant declines from:

- Nigeria - 15% decline
- Uganda - 19% decline.

SA's Top Source Countries where a short-stay visa is required

	Country Ranking IRO number of arrivals to SA	Percentage Decline Q1 2015/14
China	12	-38%
India	16	-13%
Nigeria	17	-15%
Angola	22	-1%
Kenya	27	-5%
DRC	28	-4%
Ghana	31	-13%
South Korea	36	-35%
Uganda	40	-19%
Philippines	41	0%
Russia	43	-47%
Taiwan	45	-32%

Bac says that during the first quarter of 2009, when the world was in deep recession, South Africa recorded a 2.5% drop in tourist arrivals for the same period.

"When comparing our recessional years to our current situation, it's a big shock."

South Africa has rarely experienced any decline in tourism arrivals since 1994. Small declines were recorded in the first quarter of 2004 (-0.8%) and there was a decline of 0.6% during the first three months of 2001.

"Based on global tourism forecasts for 2015, South Africa should not be experiencing these levels of decline" says Bac. "South Africa appears to be 'bucking the global trend' at the moment."

She cautions that there will be far reaching implications resulting from this dramatic decline, and most notably a price squeeze will result as tourism product owners fight for a shrinking foreign tourism market and a price sensitive domestic market.

"There will most definitely also be job losses especially in niche tourism operators that focus on specific foreign tourism markets i.e. China and India," Bac continues.

Bac adds that the recent Xenophobic attacks in South Africa are not to blame for the decrease in foreign arrivals because these only flared up towards the end of the first quarter this year, which was after the period under review.

"The decline could be attributed in part to the aftermath of the Ebola virus which affected West Africa," says Bac. "But one of the other factors has to be South Africa's new immigration regulations which now require foreign tourists who need a visa to visit South Africa to appear 'in person' and submit biometric data when applying for a Visa."

The new Visa requirements, came into effect on 1 October 2014. But requiring biometrics as part of a visa application is a fairly standard request around the world.

"The problem with South Africa's biometric visa legislation is that the infrastructure was not in place around the world when the law came into effect and communication around implementation and the requirements was unclear. This caused confusion and complications in the market," says Bac. "Some markets have retaliated because of this – and now South Africa is getting less marketing and brochure space in the travel advertising world as a result. The issue is not about submitting biometrics or appearing in person for a visa. It's about the lack of systems to do so easily and simply. When applying for a visa it's often a tourist's first point of contact with South Africa and it is important that we remain a welcoming destination."

"At a time when the world is getting more 'friendly' with travel regulations, while maintaining legislative requirements where necessary, we seem to be going in the opposite direction with our disorganisation, lack of systems and added boundaries. One can only imagine what the new Birth Certificate legislation will do to our arrivals in the coming months, since its implementation came into effect on 1 June this year," Bac concludes. **it**

WYSTC 2015 CAPE TOWN
22-25 SEPTEMBER • SOUTH AFRICA

The essential global youth travel industry event

REGISTER NOW

GROW YOUR BUSINESS
IN THE GLOBAL YOUTH TRAVEL INDUSTRY

Now in its 24th year, the World Youth and Student Travel Conference - WYSTC 2015 - is the must-attend business-to-business trade conference for key stakeholders and organisations working in youth, student and educational travel.

It's the first time that WYSTC will be held on the African continent and we won't be back for a while, so don't miss the opportunity to meet with **over 600 industry professionals** representing more than **450 organisations** across **120 countries** at the Cape Town International Convention Centre this September.

Register now at www.wystc.org

Tap in to the thriving youth travel industry

Take part in pre-scheduled business appointments

Gain the latest insights

JOIN WYSE TRAVEL CONFEDERATION AND SAVE!

Our members **save EUR 600 per delegate** on WYSTC 2015 registration.

You will also benefit from being part of the world's largest and most powerful network of youth, student and educational travel operators, which serves **over 30 million** young travellers each year.

Visit **www.wysetc.org** for more information and to join.

- Comprehensive seminar and workshop programme
- Meet hosted buyers from across the globe
- Sponsorship and exhibitor packages
- Global Youth Travel Awards
- Networking events

 /wystc   **@WYSTC | #WYSTC2015**   **www.wystc.org**

WYSTC is the annual event of **WYSE TRAVEL CONFEDERATION**

2015 Lilizela Tourism Awards Judging Begins

Earlier this year, South African Tourism invited members of the tourism industry to form part of the 2015 Lilizela Tourism Awards adjudication panel. This invitation was well-received, with the cream of the industry offering to do service on the Lilizela panel of judges, writes **Des Langkilde**.

Adjudicating the 2015 Lilizela Tourism Award entries is not an easy task. I know this from both current and past experience, having participated as a judge for the 2014 awards in the 'Service Excellence - Visitor Experience' category.

The judging process started in May, when 23 *(see image below)* of the 46 appointed judges gathered at the Protea OR Tambo Hotel on an unusually warm highveld Thursday for an orientation briefing, which was professionally coordinated and chaired by South African Tourism staff (who have asked to remain anonymous). The balance of the judges were briefed individually.

After a round of introductions and signing of nondisclosure agreements *(which is hard for a journalist to do, and why no secrets are disclosed here)*, the convener proceeded to lay down the rules and run through the judging processes and procedures under the watchful eye of auditors from Grant Thornton.

After a laborious process of remote (online) judging in June, my group reconvened at The Lakes Hotel & Conference Centre in July to debate the final scores, from which finalists, provincial winners and national winners were determined.

The final results recognise the best of the best of business owners and service providers who uphold service of excellence in their day to day operations. Launched in 2013, the awards have helped bolster South Africa's reputation as a destination of excellence and variety across all experiences and accommodation types.

As Thulani Nzima, Chief Executive Officer at South African Tourism says; "The 46 people who have been selected to adjudicate bring gravitas to the Awards. Their role as judges confirms the credibility of the Lilizela Tourism Awards as the premier awards for the tourism industry, and gives us the confidence of knowing every entry will be judged by people whose commitment to excellence in tourism is absolute. The judges also play a pivotal part in ensuring continuous collaboration in the tourism industry. Through the time they give to these awards, they bring the benefit of their experience and expertise to this national quest to find, and acknowledge, that best of the best in our tourism industry. They earn the deep gratitude of South African Tourism and of the larger travel and tourism sector."

I certainly concur with Thulani, and have to add that the award selection process has been handled with an incredible degree of professionalism and transparency. I look forward to the imminent gala award ceremonies and winner announcements.

The Provincial Awards Ceremonies will take place in September, and the National Awards on 22 October 2015 in Johannesburg. **it**

A few of the 2015 Lilizela Award Judges.

Standing (left to right): **Jaya Naidoo** - *Durban University of Technology*, **Nesang Maleka & Ntokozo Luvuno** - *both from SA Youth in Travel, Tourism & Hospitality*, **Yolande Le Roux** - *T-Cup*, **Des Langkilde** - *Tourism Tattler*, **Alex Adjei** - *Responsible Tourism Trainer*, **Barry Clemens** - *Selborne Hotel, Golf Estate & Spa*, **Jonathan Jacobs** - *Cape Chamber of Commerce*, **Ernest Bergins** - *SANParks Addo Region*, **Kiera Schoeman** - *Urban-Econ Development Economists*, **Johannes Hatting** - *Central University of Technology: Free State*, **Rebecca Kambule** - *Hampshire Hotel*, **Jonker Fourie** - *Emfuleni Corridor Tourism*, **Roebendry Gangiah** - *Soft Touch Trading*, **Siphokazi Mjali** - *SA Youth in Travel, Tourism & Hospitality*, **Phillip Bokaba** - *Motsethabo Tours*, and **Marie Wilcox** - *XO Africa*.

Seated (left to right): **Adrienne Harris** - *Harvest Tourism*, **Hloniphile Thabethe** - *Ndalo Hotel & Conferencing*, **Loshni Naidoo** - *Grand Tourism*, **Portia Sifolo** - *Tshwane University of Technology*, **Debbie Goveia** - *TGCSA Assessor*, and **Lizzie Mokgothu** - *SATSA*.

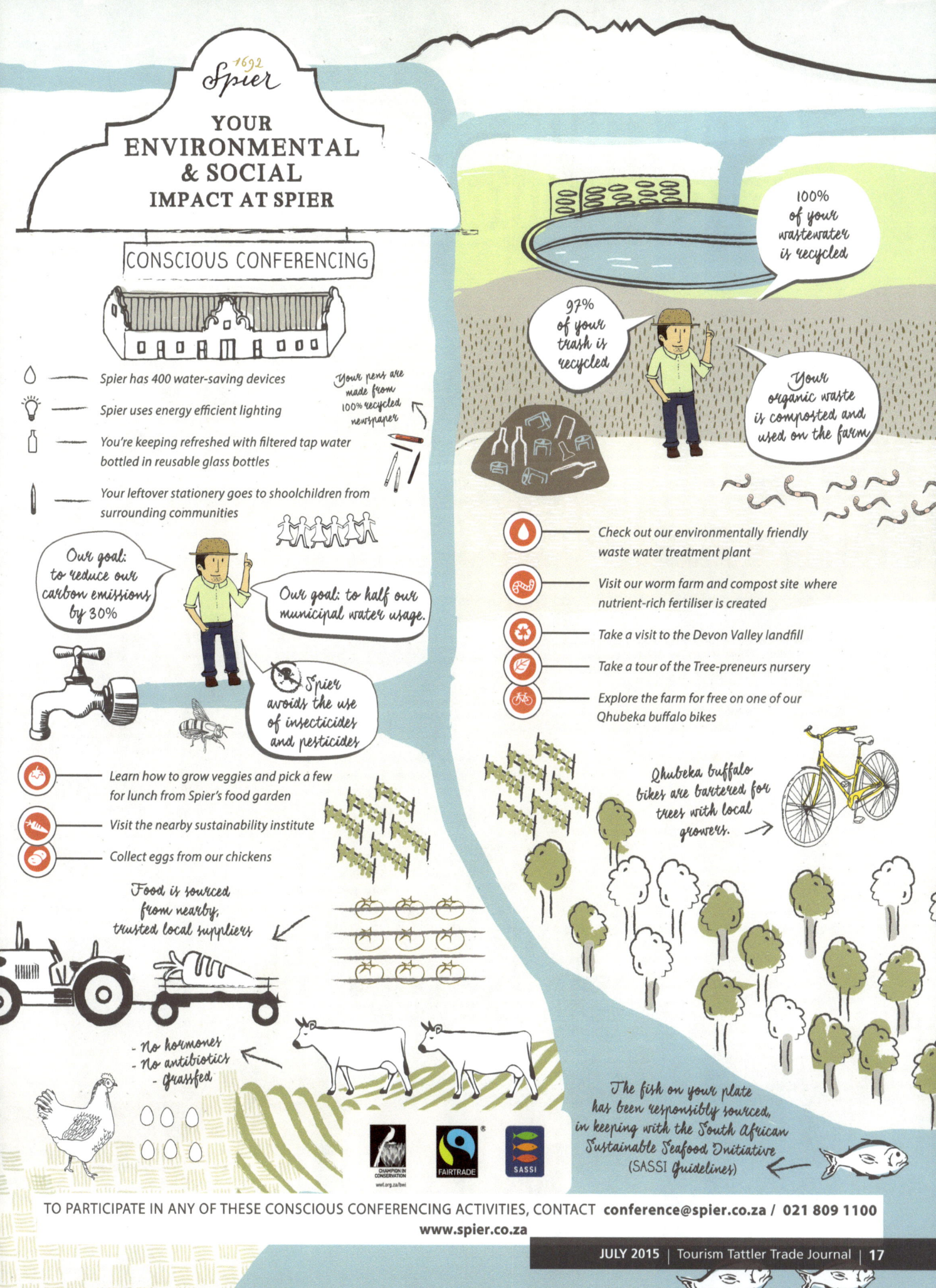

Conscious Conferencing

CONSCIOUS CONFERENCING
AT SPIER

Spier

Spier Wine Farm in Stellenbosch coined the phrase 'Conscious Conferencing'. **Des Langkilde** investigates this claim and finds it to be more than just a marketing ploy – it's an historical commitment to environmentally and socially responsible practices.

Following my Spier Venue Review in April, and Check List for Eco-Conference Venue Selection article in May, I Googled the words *'Conscious Conferencing'* and found that Spier dominates the top position *(top 3 out of 430,000 results)*. Intrigued by this result, I downloaded their CONSCIOUS CONFERENCE PACKAGE sales manual and headed off to meet with Angela Lorimer - Head of Conferencing and Eventing, and Mark Bland - Brand Manager: Leisure at Spier.

I asked how Spier justifies its 'Conscious Conferencing' claim.

"As one of the very first farms to be established in Stellenbosch in 1692, Spier has a long history – not just in viticulture, but also in farming with biodynamic principles in mind. We manage almost 300 hectares under biodynamic agricultural practices, and our ethically produced meat and vegetables are used in our farm-to-table eating experiences in our restaurants, picnic baskets and of course at our conference venues," says Mark.

"At Spier we constantly strive to find innovative ways for our business to succeed in balance with our environment and society. We call our approach to events 'Conscious Conferencing'. By hosting your event at Spier, you'll be helping us to uplift our communities, support local businesses, contribute to staff wellness and benefit our environment – all the while treating your delegates to a great experience," adds Angela.

Talking to this pair of enthusiastic managers while reclining in the hotel lounge, and seated beside a roaring log fire with creamy expresso in hand, it becomes obvious that they are both passionate and proud of their respective products and service offerings at Spier.

Steering the conversation back to the conference side, I discover that since re-launching the conference and event facilities in 2008, a great deal of effort has gone into conserving energy and reducing carbon emissions.

This has been achieved by providing alternatives to traditional conference facilities, such as using ceiling fans instead of air conditioners, providing bulk mineral water dispensers to encourage delegates to refill their own glass water bottles, and providing clearly marked bins for recyclable and non recyclable items.

In addition, Spier contributes to the local community by offering a service to conference organisers whereby they can purchase their corporate gift selections from recommended local craft associations, and donate left-over pens and notepads to schools in the area.

The conference menu selections include onsite farmed and locally produced fresh, seasonal and organic food, while leftover food is distributed to the local community.

Leaving the comfort of Spier Hotel, and the company of my hosts, I took a quick guided tour of the conference venues. Spier has 12 different meeting venues varying in capacity – from the Conference Centre to the historic Manor House, Spier can cater for large and small conferences, business meetings, workshops, seminars and exhibitions. All this on a historic wine farm, just 40 minutes from Cape Town. For more information on each of the conference venues, click here.

After arriving back at my faithful iMac desktop, I opened the interactive CONSCIOUS CONFERENCE PACKAGE sales manual, which really is a very useful tool for conference, event and exhibition planners. The PDF brochure contains everything that one would need for planning, including video links, full day and half day conference package rates, accommodation rates, food, wine, leisure (spa and craft market) and activities, and detailed specifications with seating capacities at each of the fourteen venues. **it**

Download Spier's Conscious Conference package here.

For more information visit www.spier.co.za

Speaking with Ghosts in Grahamstown

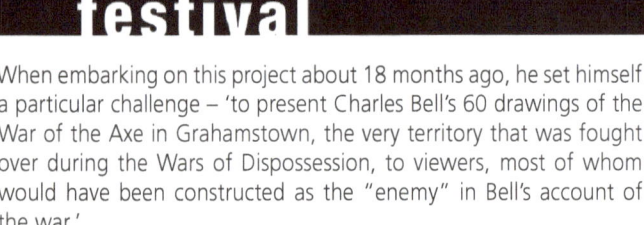

national arts festival

Playing directly into the decolonial cultural climate triggered by the Rhodes Must Fall movement, many productions at this year's National Arts Festival will be raising up the troubled ghosts of the 19th century, writes **Alexandra Dodd**.

In early March, when frustrated UCT students directed their rage at the flattering bronze of arch-colonialist Cecil John Rhodes gazing smugly down over Cape Town, Michael Godby was many months deep into the research and conceptualization of his Battleground exhibition for this year's National Arts Festival.

If South African public consciousness was not sufficiently focused on the gross crimes and misdemeanours and of the 19th century before that moment, with a single, perfectly timed swirl of excrement, the distant past was brought fiercely to life – not so much the immediate wounds, which are routinely picked at, but the deeper, older injuries underlying the scab of apartheid. In a sudden Frankenstein moment, the frame had completely changed upping the ante on Godby's challenge to himself as the curator of an already contentious show, in which he had chosen to grapple head on with the colonial wars of dispossession, a fairly early chapter in the visualization of South Africa through the eyes of Empire.

Battleground is an exhibition of 19th-century artist Charles Bell's drawings of the War of the Axe. Godby is Emeritus Professor of History of Art at the University of Cape Town, who has curated *Is there Still Life? Continuity and Change in South African Still Life Painting* (2007) and *The Lie of the Land: Representations of the South African Landscape* (2010).

'Sir Harry Darrell & Mr Gore with their troop of 7th Dragoon Guards' by Charles Bell.

When embarking on this project about 18 months ago, he set himself a particular challenge – 'to present Charles Bell's 60 drawings of the War of the Axe in Grahamstown, the very territory that was fought over during the Wars of Dispossession, to viewers, most of whom would have been constructed as the "enemy" in Bell's account of the war.'

'The idea was to find an historical context in which to situate the drawings and then to juxtapose them with recent treatments of the War and the series of wars,' he says. Not an easy task in the first place, considering that, from 1842 to 1844, a few years before the War, Bell was stationed in Grahamtown as a land surveyor adjudicating land claims which derived from 1820 Settlers – so he was actively involved in legitimating dispossession of land belonging to amaXhosa people. Born in Scotland, Bell came to South Africa when he was 16. His uncle was the colonial secretary, Sir John Bell – a military man from the Napoleonic wars. His parents don't appear to have been aristocratic, but Bell was part of a kind of colonial career aristocracy here in South Africa at the time, and was appointed Surveyor General in 1848, so although not militarily involved in the War, he had deep vested interests in the land.

Godby's aim was to interrogate the context so thoroughly that he could offer viewers an understanding of the kind of thinking that informed Bell's often caricatural depictions of Xhosa people. He traces a shift from early 19th-century depictions of Xhosa people by artists like John Barrow and Samuel Daniel, who 'seem to have regarded the Xhosa with some respect and admiration, as living free, without strife, without labour', to later depictions, by Thomas Baines and Bell, who represent them 'as people who need to be civilised – in other words, as debased'. Godby links this shift in the language of aesthetic depiction to the growth of colonial ambitions for territorial expansion – that moment in the 1840s when colonists started gazing beyond the borders of the Cape Colony and wanting land belonging to amaXhosa people.

'I'm trying to make it quite physical – to show how all of this was going on by means of maps, a sextant, title deeds, an advertisement from the Grahamstown Journal that shows a list of claimants to land, who met with Bell to have their claims adjudicated,' he says. Numerous weapons – muskets and swords – will also form part of the exhibition. 'The underlying idea is that the drawings were weapons of propaganda in the same way that the muskets and swords were weapons of war,' says Godby.

Cedric Nunn's photograph of the Grahamstown Cathedral - the site of Xhosa Chief Ndlambe's Great Kraal.

The second part of the show comprises recent representations of the War of the Axe and related Wars of Dispossession – new versions of historical events by both black and white artists, including Chumani Xonxa, Hentie van der Merwe, Paul Emmanuel, Athi-Patra Ruga, Nomusa Makhubu, Vusi Khumalo, Hilary Graham, Zola Toyi, Christine Dixie, Gabriel Clark-Brown, Keith Dietrich and Stephen Inggs.

There are likely to be some eerie moments of time collapse and haunting site-specificity as viewers wander about the Albany Museum knowing that the bloodshed took place in that very territory. 'Yes, Francki Burger's The Battle of the Gwanga is like that. She went to the site of the battle as if with a mine detector – picking up a sense of the trauma that played out there,' says Godby. 'Also Cedric Nunn's photograph of the Grahamstown Cathedral. According to Nkosi Mxolisi Hamilton Makinana, descendant of five warrior chiefs who fought against the Boers and the British in the 100 Year War of Resistance to Settler and Colonial Domination, this was the site of Ndlambe's Great Kraal. And Brent Meistre's photograph of the Egazini memorial in Fingo Village – built to symbolise reconciliation, it now stands in ruins looking out over the landscape.'

There are so many fraught ideas at work in this complex, multi-layered exhibition it's not surprising that the demise of the Rhodes bronze from its position of primacy started to intervene in Godby's curatorial thinking, keeping him up at night. 'The Rhodes Must Fall movement has made this an uncomfortable project, and I have made some changes,' he says.

The upshot is that two panels, which were initially going to be part of the exhibition will now only feature in the book. Censorship, censorship, you might cry – until you learn that the first panel grappled with the legacy of the word 'k----r', examining its use in different historical contexts and questioning whether most people in the 19th century understood it as the term of extreme offence we understand it as today. The second dealt with 19th-century racial theory, and the kinds of toxic ideas of difference as science that informed Bell's prejudiced conception of the so-called other.

'I decided against exhibiting this material, but it is in the book, which has a more academic framing and allows for differences of opinion,' says Godby. 'Hopefully, greater space, time and sensitivity can be given to it there – because Bell knew about all that stuff and his drawings of Xhosa people pulling the clothes off Captain Norden (the first white soldier to die in the war) are informed by that stuff. I cannot ignore that, but it must be presented in the right place.'

'One of the sad, and I hope, temporary consequences of the Rhodes Must Fall movement is not its ends but its means. I think it has effectively closed space for historical discussion. South Africa is a country of increasing amnesia with a tendency to flatten history, which has terrible pernicious effects. Everything gets reduced to black and white and that is not being fair or true to history. Because, for example, the Mfengu, fought on the colonial side, and occasionally the San fought on the Xhosa side. Liberated blacks and Malays fought as part of the British troops, and so on. So it was very complicated. And this stuff has got to get out there.'

If this year's Festival programme is any indication of South African culture at large, Godby's desire for nuanced, difficult narrations of the issues stirred up by the Rhodes Must Fall movement is being well met. A wide range of shows are likely to illicit spine-tingling resonances with the live-action contestations of public culture in South Africa right now.

Far from a coincidence or a knee-jerk reaction to current events, it seems that this is part of conscious programming strategy on behalf of Artistic Director Ismail Mahomed. 'In 2009, when Tony Lankester took over as CEO and I as Artistic Director of the National Arts Festival, it was a conscious artistic decision that we both shared that the Festival programme should not shy away from contentious themes but that the programme, in as much as it can be a celebration of the arts, should also be a catalyst for reflection and critique.'

Backing up this claim, Mahomed effortlessy runs through a whole spectrum of shows with a decolonial thrust, ranging from Jay Pather's Body of Evidence (2009) to Vincent Mantsoe's San (2010) to Neil Coppen's The Abnormal Load (2011) to Greg Latter's Death of a Colonialist to Mary Sibande's Long Live the Dead Queen (2013). 'Performance artist Doung Anwar Jahangeer raised the ire of many of the Eastern Cape's 1820 Settler descendants when [in 2012] he launched a city walk that grappled with Grahamstown's complex history of colonialism and violence,' he says. 'His tour, The Other Side, culminated with him covering the 1820 Settler family statue at the entrance of the 1820 Monument with ochre-coloured mud. This act was an incredibly powerful statement that challenged audiences to reflect on the city's monuments.'

'That same year, Standard Bank Young Artist Mikhael Subotzky collaborated with this year's Standard Bank Young Artist Athi-Patra Ruga to create a site-specific work, Performance Obscura, that challenged the representations of three of Grahamstown's most ▶

iconic monuments, the 1820 Settlers Monument, the Provost and the Observatory Museum. All of this happened while the city itself was contested about whether it should be celebrating its colonial founding 200 years ago in 1812.'

All of this happened long before the Rhodes Must Fall movement gained traction, he points out. 'And we now find that what we had been agitating about all these years is finally taking its place as part of a national conversation,' he says. 'Planning for this year's programme began in earnest during last year August. Had we anticipated that what we had been agitating about would become a national conversation in 2015? Yes; because despite funding challenges and threats of censorship, South African artists have not lost the ability to be reflective and visionary.

'They recognise that, despite our peaceful transition to a post-apartheid society, we have failed dismally over the past twenty years to engage with how the historical and physical environments of South Africa have yet to be transformed in order to bring about effective healing. The pot that fuelled the Rhodes Must Fall movement was boiling for a long while. It just needed to pour right over. That our programme this year is so dense with this debate is perhaps a barometer of the importance that an arts festival with a national footprint can play to articulate the mood of a nation.'

Other shows at NAF2105 navigating post/decolonial subject matter include:

The Imagined Land (World Premiere): In internationally acclaimed writer Craig Higginson's new play, directed by former Artistic Director of the Market Theatre Malcolm Purkey, a famous Zimbabwean novelist is about to undergo brain surgery. Her daughter, a literary critic studying in America, is coming home to Johannesburg to take care of her. A young biographer – also originally from Zimbabwe – arrives at the front door, requesting to write the biography of the woman who changed the course of his life. The Imagined Land is a new state of the nation play for our troubled, troubling times. How do we represent ourselves through narrative? How do we represent each other?

Red Earth Revisited: Famous Dutch puppet theatre company Speeltheater Holland Studio teamed up ASSITEJ South Africa and the Keiskamma Art Project to recreate the legendary story about day Nongqawuse, the young girl who prophesied that the Xhosa would be rid of their enemies if they killed their cattle and burned their grain and determine if she really was the cause of the disaster that ensued.

Portrait of Myself as My Father: Unflinching Harare-based dance company Tumbuka stages a production that grapples with the Zimbabwean psyche through a vigorous vocabulary of contemporary dance. Choreographed by New York-based Zimbabwean performer/choreographer Nora Chipaumire, Portrait of Myself as My Father 'celebrates masculinity, male presence and representation, the black African body and performance'.

Ngizwise: Created by two dynamic female choreographers, one from Johannesburg (Sonia Thandazile Radebe) and the other from Toronto (Jennifer Dallas), danced and sung by four powerful, male South African performers who reveal intimate stories of South Africa under apartheid, woven from the voices of the 'born free generation'. A complex work packed with images of community, power, individuality and masculinity in our globalized modern society.

Cape of Rebels: Reporters and poets. Activists and oppressors. Directed by Christopher Weare, Tony Jackman's new play explores two parallel periods of unrest: the Anglo-Boer War of 1899-1902 and the Struggle in the late 1980s-early 1990s. We meet Louis Leipoldt, then a young reporter and the formidable Marie Koopmans

Charles Bell, 'Sandili, Chief of the Amagaika' (C51).

de Wet, scourge of the British colonial authorities, and teachers-turned activists. They are part of the 'Cape Clutch', who wrote poetry underground to be published in Europe and America to tell the world what was happening to Cape Rebels at the hands of British forces…

Getting the Last Laugh on Cecil John Rhodes: Author, retired Constitutional Court Judge, member of the Constitutional Committee and National Executive Committee of the ANC, a Director of Research for the Ministry of Justice – Albie Sachs airs his views on recent events as part of Think!Fest.

Sentinel: Written by Dr Phindezwa Mnyaka, Taryn King's Sentinels intervention into the Grahamstown townscape blurs the various dichotomies out of which the location itself was borne. Sculpted figures haunt the passer-by discreetly, inviting one to engage through the act of seeing and observation, while frustrating the onlooker through a refusal of an equal relationship.

The Cenotaph of Dan Wa Moriri: Produced by Gita Pather and created by Tony Miyambo and Gerard Bester in collaboration with William Harding, The Cenotaph of Dan wa Moriri charts the unfolding of an intimate father-son relationship and examines the disappearance and reconstruction of memory to honour the intimacy of individual history. **it**

Content sponsored by Tourism Tattler in the interests of fostering the arts as a tourist attraction in South Africa.

About the author: *Dr Alexandra Dodd is an independent writer and editor whose PhD explores 19th century hauntings in contemporary South African visual culture. This piece was commissioned by the National Arts Festival.*

About the National Arts Festival: *This is an important event on the South African cultural calendar, and the biggest annual celebration of the arts on the African continent.*

Starting at the end of June/beginning of July, it runs for 11 days and is held in the small university city of Grahamstown, which is situated in the Eastern Cape, 130 km from Port Elizabeth.

For more information visit www.nationalartsfestival.co.za

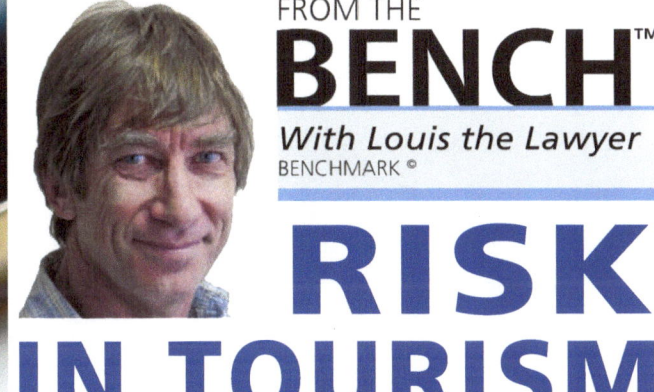

Legal

FROM THE
BENCH™
With Louis the Lawyer
BENCHMARK ©

RISK IN TOURISM
– PART 12 –
THE LAW: CONTRACTS
Signatu

REQUISITE #7: NEGOTIATING A CONTRACT

We all know by now that a contract or an agreement does not have to be in writing to be binding – a verbal contract or agreement is as binding as a written one. *So, why bother reducing it to writing?*

You may well think that this is a job creation opportunity for the legal fraternity! Allow me to share a secret with you: by drafting a detailed written agreement you may indeed be avoiding intervention by lawyers in the event of a dispute – in fact often the best agreements are concluded by lay persons avoiding 'legal speak' and simply ensuring the important issues are recorded in writing. You may be saving more than legal fees – you may be saving your business and a friendship and/or a business relationship.

Agreements come in different guises: it could be for the sale of your goods or services; it could be for the provision of goods or services to your business; it could be the appointment of an agent or sub-contractor, etc. The agreement could be negotiated afresh or based on your standard terms and conditions or that of the third party or it could be a tender or RFP/RFQ.

At the outset it is imperative that the parties have consensus about the object of the agreement: the expectations and deliverables must *'be on a par'*. Parties often 'talk past each other' on this key aspect which is the most common cause of contractual disputes. Therefore spend some time on this aspect before moving on to the rest of the agreement.

Confidentiality is an underlying requirement and prerequisite for the parties to negotiate in detail and in good faith. It is therefore good business practice for ALL parties involved in the negotiating process to sign a confidentiality, non-disclosure and non-circumvention agreement ('NDA') at an early stage. The NDA ensures that everybody is 'comfortable', there is full disclosure and avoids misunderstandings due to insufficient facts. The NDA will remain in force whether or not an ultimate contract is concluded and if it is concluded, the NDA will be incorporated as an addendum. Sometimes the non-circumvention aspect is overlooked so be sure to address it.

Ensure that the part you are negotiating with is not only a decision maker, but is also duly authorized to enter into discussions with you AND to sign the ultimate contract. It not only saves time but also lots of frustration! Establish this as early as possible in your discussions

and if there is any doubt, insist on a resolution from the legal entity the party represents or (!?) purports to represent – you may find after length discussion that you are dealing with somebody (the opposition?!) who is simply on a fact finding mission!

If there are issues of concern to either or both parties or matters that have to be resolved before an agreement can be concluded, don't 'walk away' without an agreement – simply incorporate these aspects as 'suspensive conditions' i.e. matters that have to be resolved before the agreement is of full force and effect. It does not mean the agreement is not binding but simply that its full operation is held in abeyance until these conditions are fulfilled. A typical example is the requirement of one party to raise finance or for one party to carry out a due diligence of the other.

'Talk is cheap but money buys the whisky' the saying goes. Accordingly ensure that any warranties and guarantees are reduced to writing and included in your final written agreement.

Most proposals are verbose and contain fanciful descriptions of goods and services. However, the ultimate contract you may be required to sign more often than not will include a clause stating the what you are signing is the entire agreement and that any other presentations, whether in writing or not, are excluded. Thus a disgruntled buyer may find that what he was promised by the glib salesperson and what he ultimately receives are *'worlds apart'*! Avoid this by ensuring that the glossy presentation is included in your final agreement as an addendum or at least referred to.

Likewise, when you participate in a tender ensure that your standard terms and conditions ('STC') are incorporated in your tender proposal and response to a request for a proposal/quote ('RFP'/'RFQ').

One of the problems with contract negotiations is that it can take days, weeks or sometimes months to reach final agreement. What about the interim period (when the parties sometimes [Often?!] start doing business before signing anything)? There are two things I always suggest to my clients. First of all, as suggested above, sign a NDA. Secondly, sign a letter of commitment ('LOC'). This document is also sometimes called a *'memorandum of understanding'* ('MOU') or a *'gentleman's agreement'* or a 'letter of comfort' or *'letter of intent'*. Unfortunately, if not properly worded, most of these documents end up being *'an agreement to agree'* and therefore not a binding or enforceable agreement at all. The key difference to ensure this does not result, is to have appropriate wording in the LOC stipulating inter alia that it is binding until a final agreement is signed and can also be referred to as a bridging agreement.

Why an LOC? There are various benefits, the main one being that it requires the parties to 'apply their minds' and gives them a chance to 'reassess the proposed deal'. Often a brief is given to a lawyer, a lengthy and costly contract is prepared, only for the parties to find that they actually do not want to *'do the deal'* or that, once reduced to writing, it is not really what they had in mind – and I'm not alluding to poor drafting. I simply mean that once the parties see the detail in writing and the *'bigger picture'*, it sometimes represents something *'different'*. Further benefits include giving the parties an opportunity to complete outstanding matters (e.g. suspensive conditions) by completing what I call the *'www checklist'* i.e. *'who what when'* and ownership of intellectual property is identified.

I would suggest that by applying the above principles parties are more likely to get what they want than with what they thought they wanted or were getting! it

Language: USP or Barrier?

In the hospitality and tourism industry we all try to push our unique selling points (USP's) and differentiate our products and services. Yet, how many have considered the edge language can have on the bottom line? asks **Charlene Nieuwoudt**.

"Your are invited to take advantage of the chambermaid,"

Sign in a Japanese hotel.

According to Dr Nico Nortjé, CEO of Language Inc., a South African language services company that translates 57 languages, understanding and acting on the cultural and linguistic diversity across the world is key for exceptional tourism marketing.

Linguistic ability has indeed become a valuable asset in the tourism industry – both in terms of the content of marketing material and in the creation and upkeep of a relationship with the client. The ability of staff to communicate with customers in their own languages is vital if the industry wants to flourish as customer satisfaction – and consequent positive word of mouth and return visits – very much depends on the interaction between customer and service provider. We all know how a simple 'hello, how are you' in your mother tongue can bring a smile to your face when in a foreign country.

Language is still a major barrier especially for Chinese travellers to South Africa. Their experience is that the country is ill equipped to provide tour services in their own language which forces them to bring their own tour guides. "Most of the Chinese tourists who head to Africa are not that well-versed in English," Dai Bin, President of the China Tourism Academy, was quoted as saying in a Chinese newspaper. "Unlike Europe and the US where there are lots of Chinese tourist guides and signs written in Chinese, it is rare to see Chinese signs in Africa. The language obstacle deters many Chinese customers from visiting the continent."

Tourism is an information intensive industry in which organisations rely heavily on communication with tourists through various channels to market and promote their products and build customer relationships. But surely English is the universal language of business, you say! Research will have it differently. According to Lior Cohen, vice president of Net-Translators Ltd only about 15% of the global population speaks English as a first or second language. Apparently most people around the world surf the Internet in their mother tongue. And we know that a customer's travel experience often begins online.

Which brings us to your website.

Did you know that around three quarters of the content on the Internet is in languages other than English? According to Dr Nico Nortjé additional languages take your website and consequently your reach to the next level. "Naturally you cannot accommodate the world's 7,106 languages, but you can target certain countries based on your market research and then communicate to those prospective tourist markets in their own language," he says. "Companies can begin by not only translating their website, but by localising the content (making sure the content is also culturally relevant and respectful) to provide well-translated descriptions, reviews and localised payment options."

English evidently still dominates other languages when it comes to public signs and promotional publications. Foreign languages are increasingly used by tour operations and travel agencies but the hospitality sector, including accommodation and eateries, mostly rely on English.

"While an incorrect or out of context translation – like the Japanese hotel sign – can sometimes elicit nothing more than a chuckle, such errors can have significant communication and even financial consequences for a tourist service provider," says Dr Nortjé. "The ideal is to keep language in mind when employing staff, when developing your marketing material and when conversing with your guests – even a few choice phrases will go a long way in creating a memorable experience for your guests." it

*About the author: **Charlene Nieuwoudt Communications** represents **Language Inc.** – an international language service company that is fully compliant with the EN15038 code – the world's only internationally acknowledged quality standard for translators. Language Inc. provides translation and localisation services in some 57 languages, and recently celebrated its 10th year of existence.*
For more information visit www.language-inc.org

'Expatria' a potential Tourism Source Market?

If 'Expatria' – an imaginary nation of expatriates/immigrants – were a nation, it would be the fifth most populous on the planet. In this article **William Purbrick** quantifies the demographics and size of this potential tourism source market.

Image courtesy: The Expat Survey / Shutterstock

First off, let me explain that by *'expat'* I mean anyone who lives outside of his or her nation of origin for at least six months of any twelve-month period.

By this definition, there are an estimated 232 million people living outside of their nation of origin. At The Expat Survey, we conduct independent research, and based on our 2013 survey statistics we placed the world's expatriates into an imaginary country, to determine how that country would look and feel.

Population

'Expatria' would have a population of 232 million, rising from 154 million in 1990 and 175 million in 2000, according to UN statistics. This ranks *Expatria* as the fifth most populous nation on the planet, over three and a half times the number of people in the United Kingdom and sandwiched between Indonesia and Brazil – half the population size of the European Union. *Expatria's* population growth rate of over a third since 1990 is matched by Brazil and Indonesia, two of the fastest growing economies worldwide.

The population of *Expatria* must be considered one of the most diverse on the planet. The largest proportion of people coming from South Asia, accounting for 36 million of the population, with about 19 million migrants living in Europe, some 16 million in Northern America and about 3 million in Oceania. The second and third largest groups coming from Central America and the Caribbean, 17.4 million Central Americans are living in the US.

The population of *Expatria* equates to 3.2% of the world's population but what do we really know about them?

The understanding of Expatria is in black-and-white with broad strokes, while the UN suggest a worldwide population of extra-nationals in 232 million, independent research conducted by Finaccord suggests a figure 56 million worldwide in 2014. At least there are estimates for the size of this universe, beyond quantitative figures, little is known of the quality and composition of the lives of expatriates.

Age

The average age of the citizens of *Expatria* would be 38, being at their average youngest in Africa and oldest in Oceania. UN statistics estimate that 48% of the population would be women and 26 million of the residents aged 65+ years of age and proportionally greater represented than they are in the world population, 11% of the migrant population yet just 8% of the world's population.

Interestingly, 20-34 year olds represent 64 million people and also less females, which can be attributed to the transit of male migrant workers, especially those based in Asia.

Wealth

Measuring the wealth of *Expatria* is difficult; however remittance figures estimated by the World Bank give some indicator of the economic power of expatriates worldwide. The World Bank estimates $435 billion will be sent in remittance in 2014, outweighing ODA (official development assistance) by a factor of three. Although being a crude comparison, this figure would project *Expatria* as a top 40 world economy in 2014 if taken as its GDP. This is without considering the estimated wealth of tax exiles to be found in the havens of Switzerland, Luxembourg and the like. A study conducted by economist James Henry suggests at least £13 trillion ($20tn) squirreled away worldwide, which would catapult its ranking amongst the top few.

Occupation

The citizens of *Expatria* are workers in a diverse range of fields that have significant economic power. European immigrants (European Economic Area) in the UK have contributed £20bn a year from 2001 to 2011 according to a study conducted by University College, London. Not only are expats economic contributors but work in various sectors. In the case of the UK, The Telegraph states that migrants from within the EU primarily fulfilling manual work, in factories and farming, whilst Non-EU immigrants are prominent in professional roles in health and science.

This article has highlighted that there is a massive population, globally-based, that tourism destination marketers know very little about. The findings of the Expat Survey 2013 illuminated that expatriates spend more time on sites from their country of origin rather than sites of their country of residence; 70% still choosing to shop online from native sites. The deficiency of information highlights the need for independent research, the need for the The Expat Survey. it

Sources: CIA Factbook, UN, The Guardian, The Telegraph, UCL, The Expat Survey 2013, Finaccord.

About the author: William Purbrick *is Research and Digital Assistant at London based The Expat Survey. TheExpatSurvey.com is the largest 'independent' annual research programme of those living outside their country of origin; and is a leading authority on what, when, why and how expatriates communicate and consume.*

For more information visit www.theexpatsurvey.com

Seven Tips to Improve your B2B Marketing
- Part 2 -

In the June edition of Tourism Tattler, I wrote Part One of a three-part series that outlines seven tips for B2B companies to increase the ROI on their marketing efforts, shorten the sales cycle and increase conversions. Part One of the series offered tips on how to use public relations and content marketing to promote your B2B company, and this month in Part Two, I will be covering another very important B2B marketing tactic: conferences and industry events, writes **Jennifer Nagy**.

Conferences & Industry Events

Industry conferences are a fantastic way to meet potential clients face-to-face, which helps to develop relationships much more quickly than email or phone contact alone. As such, it is more likely to make your potential customer more receptive to your sales pitch if you have already met in person.

Choose the conferences that you attend based on the ideal client that you are trying to reach. Whether you are choosing to sell to international flagged brands or small, independent hotels, there are conferences that are better suited to your specific niche.

Unless you have millions of marketing dollars at your disposal (which is becoming more and more infrequent nowadays), I would recommend only selecting only the top two to three annual conferences that will appeal to your target audience. With conferences, *'quality over quantity'* should be your mantra because it does take a significant amount of money to make your booth (and your product) stand out amongst the hundreds (or even thousands) of other suppliers attempting to reach the same audience, at the same event.

There are three options for possible involvement in industry events and conferences, and I recommend that B2B companies consider including all three at every event in which they choose to participate (if possible).

Exhibiting

Your B2B company should be exhibiting during the trade show portion of all top industry conferences. In order to stand out, create a booth with a strong brand image, as well as lots of interesting/ engaging visuals. Offer on-site demos and if possible, incentivize potential customers to come visit your booth.

Before the conference, spend a great deal of time developing collateral that will appeal specifically to the attendees of this conference. Reach out to your marketing list and invite them to arrange meetings/demos with you on-site. Consider planning an on-site event that will bring potential customers to your booth; food and cocktails are always very popular with conference attendees so if you have the budget, definitely consider organising a cocktail party or a special dinner to entice visitors to your booth.

Speaking opportunities

You should also consider applying to be a keynote speaker or participate in an expert panel at your selected conferences. This gives you the opportunity to demonstrate your expertise in your subject matter of choice, making any potential customers who are listening more apt to trust your company and consider accepting your sales pitch at a later date.

Speaking opportunities are also a great way to secure trade media coverage (I'll go into more detail on this in a moment).

In order to secure a speaking opportunity, you will need to start planning in advance of the conference.

Most conference organizers start planning the event (including keynote and panel topics and presenters) at least six months (or even up to a year) in advance. That means that you will need to apply a minimum of six months before the event to be considered for a speaking opportunity.

Check out the conference website for details on how to apply. Some conferences require a specific application package to be completed, while others simply request that you send an email outlining your proposed speech topic.

Either way, you will need to have a specific topic/angle in mind, in order to be considered. Consider what info conference attendees would need to/want to learn during the event and work your proposal around that subject matter.

The more interesting your topic to potential attendees, the more likely you will be to secure a speaking opportunity at the event.

Media outreach

Finally, conferences offer a fantastic opportunity to secure media coverage for your company and/or product/service. At most larger conferences, organizers invite trade media from around the world to attend and cover the event. Many publications even publish dedicated conference issues so they are always in need of interesting stories to share.

Not only is media exposure beneficial because it creates on-site visibility, it also helps your company to develop stronger relationships with media that will yield even greater coverage over time. Like with potential customers, it is harder to say no to someone who you've met in person so use this opportunity to meet as many journalists who cover your industry as possible.

Before starting to pitch, it is important that you decide upon an interesting angle for your company's presence at the event. Are you launching a new product? Have you moved in a new strategic direction? Are you planning an interesting/fun event at your booth? Is your product changing the way that hotels operate? All of these angles could interest media to come interview your company's spokesperson on-site.

Reach out to the event organizers at least a month before the event and ask if they would be willing to share the list of confirmed media attendees. In most cases, the event organizers are happy to share this info, especially with their confirmed exhibitors. Also, ask the organizers about their process for issuing media passes to the event. Once you have the list, reach out to each journalist with a short email introducing your company and product/service, and outlining your unique story angle. Invite them to come by your booth and meet with you and/or view a product demo.

If you have an international trade media list (or you work with a PR firm who does), reach out to all other media to find out if they are planning the conference, and if not, invite them to attend. Offer to secure them a media pass to the event (which can be obtained from the conference organizers). The few minutes that it takes to secure their media pass can be highly beneficial; journalists are much more likely to book an interview and run a story about your company when you've helped them out.

If you can, confirm a time for the media interview in advance of the conference because journalists' schedules do fill up quickly. To keep organized, create a schedule for your spokesperson, which includes all pertinent information about each interview (i.e. outlet name and description, name and contact info of journalist, angle of story, demo request, etc.) and keep it updated as new media interviews are added.

You should also prepare any necessary visuals (i.e. images, headshots, videos, press kits, etc.) in advance in case journalist on a short deadline requests one. This brings me to an important point: media who are covering industry events and conferences are typically on a VERY short deadline – sometimes, as short as a few hours. As I mentioned, many publications release daily conference issues so in order to capitalize on the visibility offered by an article published during the event (which can drastically increase foot traffic to your booth), you must be prepared well in advance. **it**

About the author: Jennifer Nagy is the President of JLNPR, a full-service public relations and marketing agency that lives and breathes all facets of the travel technology industry. From online travel agencies to revenue management systems, tablet-based aviation automation solutions to IFE technology, hotels to airlines and everything in between, JLNPR uses our knowledge and experience to get your B2B travel technology company noticed by media, influencers and potential customers. JLNPR creates stories and trends around clients' news, providing journalists with every resource they could need to write the story. It is a philosophy that has served our clients well, as we are consistently able to secure high-profile media coverage on their behalf.

To find out more about JLNPR visit www.jlnpr.com or contact Jennifer at jenn@jlnpr.com

www.ingramcontent.com/pod-product-compliance
Lightning Source LLC
Chambersburg PA
CBHW050431180526
45159CB00005B/2490

* 9 7 8 1 5 1 5 0 1 7 9 2 9 *